CCSS Genre Fiction

Essential Question
How do people get along?

by Jerome Anderson
illustrated by Jesse Graber

Coming to Visit

"The cousins are coming!" Meg shouted as she ran into the kitchen.

"Yes, the cousins are coming today," Mom said. She looked amused. "I can see you're excited about that."

"Well, I'm not," Ben said from his place at the table. "I have to sleep on the floor in the living room with two other boys. I wouldn't describe that as fun."

"The girls get to sleep in my room with me!" Meg said. "Where will the aunts and uncles sleep?" she asked.

"They will sleep in the guest room and in Ben's room," Mom said. "We have plenty of space for all of us."

"Can't I sleep over at Matt's house?" Ben begged. "His mom said it was okay."

3

"We already told you no," Dad said. "I know it's going to be a little crowded, but I think you will have fun with your cousins."

Ben frowned. "I don't see how," he said. "What if they don't want to do what I want to do? Why do they have to stay here anyway?"

"You're on thin ice, Ben," Mom warned. "I don't want to hear another complaint. I expect you to be nice and to cooperate. Now, go help Dad get the sleeping bags out."

Ben knew better than to say anything else. Mom was excited to see the family. Dad and Meg were excited, too. Ben was the only one dreading the visit.

He didn't want to sleep on the floor. He didn't want to play with a bunch of little kids. And what if the baby cried all night? He liked his quiet, peaceful house just the way it was.

CHAPTER 2

Everyone Is Here

After he helped Dad get ready, Ben went back to his room. *I should enjoy the quiet now,* he thought. But just a few minutes later he heard a car door slam.

Meg ran down the hall yelling, "They're here!"

Slowly, Ben walked out to the front yard. His family rushed to meet Aunt Anna and Uncle Tony and their girls.

Another car pulled into the driveway. Out of this one came Aunt Sue, Uncle Carlos, and their boys.

Everyone hugged and kissed and smiled. Ben's baby cousin waved and clapped. The girls ran in circles around the yard, giggling. Ben counted. *Twelve people having fun,* he thought. *And me.*

Ben stood at the edge of the yard thinking, *They sure make a lot of noise.* Then he noticed his cousin Alex on the opposite side of the yard. They were about the same age, Ben remembered. Alex looked as unhappy as Ben felt.

8

CHAPTER 3

Let's Play

Ben thought about what Dad and Mom had said about being nice. He took a deep breath and called, "Hey, Alex! Want to go play soccer in the back yard?"

Alex looked up and grinned. "Yes! I love soccer! I had to miss my game today to come here."

"I had to miss *my* game today because you were coming," Ben said. "Come on, let's go before they say we have to keep the little kids entertained!"

Ben led the way to the back yard. The boys played soccer. Meanwhile, the rest of the family got settled.

It didn't take long for the girls and Alex's little brother to find them.

"Can we play?" Meg said.

"No," Ben and Alex said at the same time. They laughed, but then Ben said, "I guess we do need to play with them."

"Yeah," Alex said. "My parents said I had to include my brother and the girls."

"Mine said I had to be nice and cooperate," Ben said. "Let's think of something we can all play together."

CHAPTER 4

Not So Bad

The rest of the afternoon passed quickly as the cousins played in the backyard. Soon, Mom was calling them in for pizza.

As the family crowded around laughing and joking together, Dad pulled Ben aside. "You're doing great," Dad said. "I like the way you used your imagination and played games with the little kids. You were very patient."

Ben said, "It's not so bad. I might even have some old toys in my room that they can play with later."

"You can bring those out tomorrow," Dad said. "It's about time for the little ones to hit the hay. But you and Alex can stay up for a while."

Ben smiled. He listened to his happy family talking around him. Alex pointed to the seat he had saved for Ben.

Maybe thirteen wasn't such a crowd after all.

Respond to Reading

Summarize

Use details to help you summarize *Thirteen Is a Crowd.*

Character	Clue	Point of View

Text Evidence

1. How do you know *Thirteen Is a Crowd* is fiction? Genre

2. What does Ben think about his cousins visiting in the first part of the story? How do you know? Point of View

3. Use context clues to figure out what "hit the hay" means on page 14. Idioms

4. Write about how Ben changes by the end of the story. Give details.

   Write About Reading

Compare Texts
Read about a group that helps kids of all ages.

Big Brothers Big Sisters

Some kids have a big brother or big sister in their family. Other kids have a different kind of Big Brother or Big Sister.

Big Brothers Big Sisters is a nationwide group that matches Bigs with Littles. Bigs are adult mentors. They volunteer to help and guide kids. Littles are kids ages 6 to 18 who need an adult friend.

Bigs and Littles do many interesting activities together.

Sometimes Bigs help their Littles with schoolwork.

Big Brothers Big Sisters has been working to help kids have better lives for more than 100 years. Bigs act as role models for the Littles. They help the Littles make good choices.

Big Brothers started in New York City in 1904. A court clerk asked for someone to volunteer to be "a big brother" to a boy who needed help.

Bigs and Littles interact in all kinds of ways. Each match is different, but the goal is always the same. Every Big wants his or her Little to have a great life.

Bigs and Littles play together, too.

Make Connections

Why is it important to get along with your family? Essential Question

How do both stories show people getting along? Text to Text

Focus on
Social Studies

Purpose To find out why it is important to cooperate

What to Do

Step 1 ▶ Find out about a group in your community that helps people get along together. It might be a group you are already part of, like a team or a scout troop.

Step 2 ▶ Write a paragraph telling about the group. Tell what it does and how it helps people get along. Include any other details that show how the group is special.